Fly, Sam, Fly!

Author: Travis Dorsch
Illustrator: Breanna Studenka

Copyright © 2025

Travis Dorsch and Breanna Studenka

ALL RIGHTS RESERVED. NO part of this book may be reproduced or transmitted in any form by any means, electronic or mechanical, including photocopying and recording, or by any information storage and retrieval system, except as may be expressly permitted in writing from the author.

ISBN: 978-1-966968-54-2

Published by:

www.owlpublishers.com

360 S Market St, San Jose, CA 95113,

United States.

Printed in the United States of America

Dedication

By Skylar Jackenthal

To my brother Sam,

Whose joy, kindness, and courage still soar through every mountain, every heart,

and every dream in our community.

May every child who reads this book be inspired to fly like you - by lifting others up,

taking bold risks, chasing wild dreams, and smiling each day.

Fly, Sam, Fly!

BOOK DESCRIPTION

Fly, Sam, Fly! is an inspiring children's story that follows the adventures of a young skier named Sam, whose courage, joy, and kindness uplift his mountain community. From conquering the towering slopes of Monster Peak to discovering the power of friendship, leadership, and resilience, Sam learns that bravery isn't about being fearless — it's about trying, even when it's hard. Filled with snowy adventures, heartfelt lessons, and moments of laughter and love, this book encourages children to be brave, embrace joy, stay true to themselves, practice kindness, and rise stronger after every fall. Sam's story reminds readers that every mountain can be climbed, every setback can be overcome, and every child has the power to soar!

CHAPTER 1: COURAGE

Once upon a time, in a snowy mountain village, there lived a boy named Sam who loved to ski. Sam wasn't very big, but he was strong, full of energy, and loved ripping down the hills on his skis. His biggest dream was to ski down the tallest mountain near his village, Monster Peak.

Although Sam was a skilled skier, Monster Peak made him nervous. Every time he looked at it from his bedroom window, his heart raced, and he felt butterflies in his stomach.

One snowy day, Sam's coach, Jason, saw him looking up at Monster Peak from the base of the mountain.

"Thinking about skiing down the peak?" Jason asked Sam with a friendly smile.

Sam nodded shyly. "But I don't think I'm ready. It's really steep, and ... what if I fall?"

Coach Jason knelt down to be eye-level with Sam. "You know, Sam, it's okay to be scared. Being brave doesn't mean you're not scared. It means you try your hardest — even when you *are* scared."

Sam thought about what Jason said. "So ... if I try something that scares me, I'm being brave?"

"Exactly!" Jason smiled. "What matters most is whether *you* believe you can ski down that peak."

Sam started practicing on larger and steeper runs. With every lap, he felt a little braver. He learned how to stay balanced, make quick turns, and even catch some air! Each day, he got more confident. Soon, he would be ready to face Monster Peak.

Later that week, Sam spotted a bird sitting on a rock near the top of the peak. The bird looked a little nervous, just like Sam sometimes felt. But suddenly, the bird took a deep breath, jumped, and spread its wings. It soared high into the sky!

Sam felt a spark of motivation in his chest. "If that little bird can be brave ... then I can be brave too!"

The next day, with his friends Joe and Alex beside him, Sam rode the chairlift to the top of Monster Peak. He looked down and the slope was steep — and definitely scary — but he remembered what Coach Jason had told him.

"I don't have to be fearless," Sam whispered to himself. "I just have to try."

He took a deep breath and pushed off, just like he had seen the bird do the day before. The wind whooshed past him as he zipped down from the top of the peak. It was steeper than he expected, but he leaned forward and believed in himself. Halfway down, he hit a jump and soared into the air, higher than he'd ever gone before!

When he reached the bottom, Joe and Alex shouted, "You did it, Sam!" Sam grinned and gave his friends big high-fives. He was still a little scared, but he had learned an important lesson that day: every time he faced a fear, it got smaller, and his courage grew bigger.

From that day forward, Sam knew he could take on even the tallest and scariest mountains, one brave step at a time.

CHAPTER 2: JOY

The next day, Sam woke up, bundled into some warm clothes, and clicked into his skis. He was ready for another adventure! He had been practicing cool tricks like corks, backflips, and 720s to get ready for his next competition, but today was different. Today, he just wanted to explore, have fun, and follow his heart.

Sam had faced his fears on Monster Peak and now he was looking for something new: *joy*. He didn't know exactly where he would find it, but he was sure it was out there, waiting for him.

As Sam started down the mountain on his first run, a cool breeze brushed his cheeks, and the sun warmed them from above. He couldn't help but smile. "This feels amazing!" he said out loud.

At the bottom of the run, Sam saw his friends Jack and Dakota making snow angels and building an igloo. He couldn't wait to join them! Sam dove into the soft snow and started moving his arms and legs to make the biggest, fluffiest snow angel ever. As he lay back and looked up at the sky, Sam's heart filled with happiness. "There's nothing better than best friends playing in the snow!" he thought, grinning from ear to ear.

After lunch, Sam decided to try something he had never done before: a helicopter spin while skiing down a smooth, easy slope. He started with a small turn, then lifted one ski off the snow just for fun. Suddenly, he was spinning around on one ski, laughing so hard that he almost fell over! His laughter echoed from the mountains to the village.

"Trying new things makes you feel good about yourself," Sam thought as he steadied himself, feeling a happy flutter in his chest.

Back home that afternoon, Sam and his dog, Flip, climbed a small hill outside the village. Sam found a soft patch of snow to sit and looked around at the wintery landscape, glowing with a warm light. As the sun began to set behind Monster Peak, Flip curled up at his feet.

Sam felt peaceful as he watched a few gentle snowflakes float down around him, sparkling like tiny diamonds in the last bits of sunlight.

"Joy is everywhere," Sam thought to himself. "It's in the snow, the mountains, the people and furry friends you love, and in the quiet moments by yourself, too."

With his heart full of warmth and his cheeks pink from laughing and playing all day, Sam hiked slowly back home with Flip at his side. That night, as he lay in bed, he thought about all the joyful moments he had found while exploring and playing in the mountains.

He knew that no matter where he went or what he did, joy was always close by, waiting to be found.

CHAPTER 3: SELF-AWARENESS

The next morning was quiet and peaceful, with a fresh coat of snow covering the roofs in the village. Sam had already learned how to be brave and find joy in all his adventures. But today, Sam was going to learn something important about himself.

Sam's adventure began when Coach Jason invited him to a special skiing challenge called *The Spiegel*. Although Sam had heard his older friends and teammates talk about The Spiegel, he had never tried it himself.

"What's The Spiegel?" Sam asked.

"It's a race against yourself," Coach Jason explained. "The goal isn't to go the fastest or jump the highest. It's about understanding how you feel when you're on the mountain. It's about noticing how you move, what makes you feel strong, and knowing what you want to get better at."

"So, um, there's no winner?" Sam asked, his smile tinged with confusion.

Still uncertain, he decided to give it a try. He put on his skis, took a deep breath, and glided down the gentle course.

At first, Sam just focused on moving forward. But then, he remembered Coach Jason's words: "Notice *how* you ski, not how fast you ski."

So, Sam paid attention to how he shifted his weight with each turn and how his arms helped him keep balance when he jumped through the air. He realized that when he stayed calm and focused, his movements were smooth and steady. But when he started to rush, he'd sometimes wobble, feel confused, or lose his balance.

Sam stopped halfway down the run. "I think I ski better when I'm calm," he thought. "So why do I rush?"

After finishing The Spiegel, Sam looked back at the course and realized something important. When he rushed, it was because he was worried about what other people thought or because he wanted to be better than his competitors. He wasn't skiing for himself; he was skiing to impress other people.

Right then, Sam made a promise to himself: he would ski the rest of the season for the joy it brought him. He leaned into each turn, soared gracefully through the air, and let go of all the worries he had about winning.

He developed his own style — gentle, carefree, and steady. It felt amazing to ski in a way that was true to him. "It's not always about winning; it's about the dance with the snow!" he shouted to Coach Jason.

"You got it, Sam," Jason said with a proud smile. "You can learn a lot when you ski for yourself! Knowing who you are and what makes you feel good is the first step to being the best version of yourself."

Throughout the rest of winter, whenever Sam felt nervous, he took a deep breath, skied at his own pace, and tried not to worry about how fast or fancy he looked to anyone else. Each time he skied, he felt more confident, more comfortable, and more like *himself*.

CHAPTER 4: KINDNESS

Although Sam loved skiing the snowy slopes of Monster Peak, his heart reached far beyond the mountains. Sam's kindness wasn't just for skiing; he carried it with him everywhere he went.

On his first day of the new semester, Sam walked into his classroom and saw his friend Nate with his head down on the desk. Sam knew that Nate often felt shy and quiet around new people. Without hesitation, Sam walked over and gave Nate a friendly smile, hoping to make him feel better.

"Hi, Nate!" Sam said. "Wanna play with me at recess today?"

Nate looked up, surprised. "Really? That'd be great!" he said excitedly.

Sam felt happy knowing he had made Nate's day a little brighter just by being a friend. His small act of kindness had already made a big difference.

Later in the day, Sam spotted his classmate Marin struggling to carry her books. Her legs were wobbling as she tried to carry a giant stack, and it looked like she might tip over at any moment.

"Need some help, Marin?" Sam asked, stepping in with a grin. Marin sighed with relief. "Yes, please! My new textbooks are so heavy."

Sam took half of the books and walked with Marin down the hall. As they walked, they laughed and chatted, making the walk to the library much more fun. When they got there, Marin gave Sam a big hug. "Thanks, Sam! You're always so helpful."

"No big deal," Sam said. But he felt warm inside, knowing he'd made things a little easier for his friends that day.

Later that afternoon, Sam's teacher, Mrs. Johnson, asked the students to make cards for children at the village hospital. Sam was excited! He loved being creative and knew that something as simple as a kind word or colorful picture could brighten someone's day. He grabbed his colored pencils and got to work.

Sam put his heart into the cards, drawing bright, happy pictures and writing kind messages like, "You're amazing just the way you are!" and "Sending you snowy hugs from Monster Peak!"

He even encouraged the class to make extra cards so every kid at the hospital would get one.

When class was over, Mrs. Johnson looked at the stack of colorful cards. "Wow, Sam, you and your classmates really put in a lot of effort here. Thank you for making the cards extra special!"

Sam beamed. He felt proud that a small act of kindness, doing something he loved, would bring joy to other children in the village.

When Sam got home from school, he noticed his little sister Skylar staring at her spelling test. She looked sad, and Sam could tell she hadn't done as well as she'd hoped.

"It's okay, Skye," Sam said gently as he wrapped his arm around her shoulder. "Spelling is hard for a lot of people. I bet you'll do better next time. Want to practice together tonight?"

Skylar's face brightened. "That'd be awesome, Sam. Thanks for believing in me. Kindness is your superpower!"

Sam knew that kindness wasn't just about big gestures; sometimes, it was simply offering encouragement or sharing a smile with a classmate or family member. Even small words could help someone feel big inside.

At dinner, he thought about all the little ways he'd helped people that day. It made him realize that being kind at school and at home was just as important as being kind on the mountain. Kindness was like a ripple in a pond. Each small act spread out and made the world a better place.

And the best part? Anyone could do it anytime, anywhere.

As Sam went to bed that night, he made a promise to himself. No matter where he went or what he did in life, he would always look for small ways to be kind to others.

Sam knew that kindness, just like his love of skiing, was something he wanted to carry with him everywhere he went and for as long as he lived.

CHAPTER 5: LEADERSHIP

Sam was known for his courage, joy, self-awareness, and kindness. But this weekend, Sam was going to learn what it really meant to be a leader.

As Sam was preparing for a day of powder skiing with his team, he heard about a problem in the village. The annual Winter Festival was just a day away, but the big snowstorm had knocked down all the decorations, scattered signs, and left piles of snow blocking the sidewalks.

"We have to do something," Sam said as his team gathered for practice. "Without our help, the festival might have to be canceled."

Sam's heart sank. The Winter Festival was everyone's favorite event of the season, with ice skating, hot cocoa, carnival games, and music. It brought the whole village together. He couldn't imagine it being canceled.

Sam thought for a moment, then felt a spark of determination. "We can help!" he said to his teammates. "And maybe we can get others to help, too."

He shared his plan: "If we all work together, I bet we can fix things up in time for the festival," Sam told the group with a hopeful smile.

His teammates agreed, and soon word began to spread around the village. People of all ages gathered at the town square, ready to help! Sam was amazed! But he also realized there was a lot to organize. Who would step up to take charge?

Taking a deep breath, Sam decided to lead the town's effort. "Alright, everyone! Let's make a plan!" he said, gaining confidence with each word.

He gathered his teammates and the other villagers, splitting them into groups. Some kids and adults shoveled snow to clear paths, while others fixed the decorations. Sam noticed that a few of his teammates were unsure about what to do, so he took the time to show them how to hang lights and organize decorations. Another group arranged the carnival games, including his favorite, "The Claw."

"Great job, everyone!" Sam exclaimed. "We're going to get this done together!"

As the afternoon shadows grew longer, Sam noticed that some of his teammates were getting tired, and a few even wanted to go home. But Sam kept encouraging everyone, reminding them of how fun the festival would be the next day.

"Let's take a snack break!" he said, passing out hot cocoa and cookies his mom and dad had brought. "We're almost done! Thanks for sticking with it, everyone."

The warmth and cheer lifted everyone's spirits, and soon enough, the village looked ready for the festival. The sidewalks were clear, the decorations were hung, and the lights sparkled in the trees. Everyone looked around proudly, knowing they'd helped make it happen.

When the Winter Festival kicked off the next day, the whole community gathered in the village square. Sam watched as his friends and family laughed, played, and enjoyed the decorations and games. People were happy, and Sam and his teammates felt a sense of pride.

As the festival wrapped up that evening, Mr. Williams, the village's mayor, came over to Sam's family. "Sam," he said, "you brought everyone together and showed us all what it means to be a leader. You didn't just tell us what to do; you helped, you encouraged, and you made sure everyone felt like part of the team. Well done!"

Sam's cheeks turned red. He'd never thought of himself as a leader before. He just wanted to help. But now he understood that being a leader wasn't about being in charge; it was about inspiring others and making sure everyone felt valued.

True leadership, he realized, was about lifting others up, one snowy step at a time.

CHAPTER 6: RESILIENCE

The next weekend was Sam's first competition of the winter. The mountain was buzzing with energy as Sam stood at the top of Monster Peak. The crisp air carried the sounds of nervous skiers and the excitement of the crowd below. Sam had crashed during his warm-up run and was nervous about how the race would go. As he prepared to start, doubt started to creep into his mind: what if he crashed again? What if he let everyone down?

Sam's new coach, Hatch, gave Sam's shoulder a reassuring squeeze. Sam turned and asked, "Do you think I can do it, coach?"

With a wry smile, Hatch replied, "I don't know, *can* you?"

Sam knew, in that moment, that his fate was up to him and no one else.

"Remember, Sam: resilience isn't about never falling. It's about getting back up and being stronger *after* you fail."

But Sam couldn't keep his mind from replaying the crash. He had hit a patch of ice, lost control, and tumbled into the snow. Facing the challenge ahead, he took a deep breath, exhaled, and cleared his mind. He was determined to prove to himself that he could soar after a setback.

Sam spotted his family waiting anxiously near the finish line, bundled up in warm coats. His mom waved, his dad cupped his hands around his mouth to cheer, and his sister squinted to catch a glimpse of her hero through the morning sun. His family's unwavering support reminded him that no matter what happened today, they would be proud of his effort.

When it was his turn, Sam launched forward, his skis slicing through the snow. He leaned into his turns, feeling the familiar rhythm of a slope he had skied hundreds of times with Jason and Hatch. Icy patches lurked beneath the surface, but instead of fearing them, he adjusted, keeping his movements fast and strong. His body remembered the countless hours of training with his coaches and teammates. Time seemed to slow down. The sounds faded away. There was nothing else that mattered but Sam's dance with the snow.

As he neared the final jump, the crowd at the finish line erupted into cheers. "Fly, Sam, Fly! Fly, Sam, Fly! Fly, Sam, Fly!" they chanted, their voices ringing at the base of Monster Peak. Sam's heart was pounding. With a final push, he flew off the last jump, soaring high above the crowd, flipping through the air. He landed perfectly, crossed the finish line, and stopped in a spray of snow. Moments later, the scoreboard flashed — the best score of the day!

A rush of pride flooded Sam as his teammates ran to greet him. Coach Hatch clapped from the top of the course, thinking, "Atta boy, Sam. You didn't let the past define you. You faced your fears head-on and conquered them."

As Sam caught his breath, his family came toward him, their faces beaming. His mom pulled him into a hug. "We're so proud of you, Sam." His dad ruffled his helmet. "That was some incredible skiing, son. You showed amazing resilience out there." Skylar gave him a hug and smiled proudly at the cheering crowd.

Sam grinned, his heart still pounding fast. The fall during warm-ups had been part of his journey, but it hadn't defined the day. He had learned that true strength wasn't about avoiding failure — it was about rising up, stronger than before. "Falling is *learning*," he thought, "not *failing!*"

About the Author

Dr. Travis Dorsch is a professor at Utah State University, where he started the Families in Sport Lab. He and his students study how different people and situations influence young athletes' experiences, attitudes, and behaviors in youth sports. Dr. Dorsch works with organizations like the United States Olympic and Paralympic Committee, the NCAA, and the Aspen Institute to make sports better for kids. He has authored more than 70 articles and book chapters and is a former member of the national science board for the President's Council on Sports, Fitness, & Nutrition. Dr. Dorsch is also a research fellow for the U.S. Center for Mental Health & Sport and has been a member of the Live Like Sam Board of Directors since its inception in 2022.

About the Illustrator

Dr. Breanna Studenka is a professor at Utah State University, where she studies how people plan and control their movements. She's especially interested in how these abilities change as people grow, age, or face challenges like injuries or disabilities. Dr. Studenka's love for art began early—nurtured by her father, a junior high and high school art teacher, and her mother, a multifaceted artist who filled their home with fabric, paint, and projects of all kinds. Breanna has long balanced her scientific career with a deep love of storytelling and visual expression. A longtime collector and lover of children's literature, Dr. Studenka is especially drawn to books that convey life lessons through the lens of sport and movement. One of her lifelong dreams was always to write and illustrate her own children's books—stories that blend science, play, and purpose to inspire young readers to move, explore, and imagine.

About Live Like Sam

Live Like Sam is a non-profit organization based in Park City, Utah that honors the short life and legacy of Sam Jackenthal. Sam was the United States men's junior national freestyle ski champion in 2015. The next summer, Sam suffered a life-ending injury from a ski accident while training in Australia. Sam's father Ron and younger sister, Skylar launched Live Like Sam in his honor in 2019. The organization provides essential programming to over 4000 youth in kindergarten through 12th grade every year, inspiring them to develop self-awareness, courage, leadership, kindness, resilience, and joy through life skills training and character development. The foundation is committed to strengthening the development of local youth with its programs and scholarships, and to fostering a dedication to service to others ... in short, to live like Sam lived!

The foundation relies on donations for support. DONATE HERE →

Thank you for your support and remember to **Live Like Sam**!

www.ingramcontent.com/pod-product-compliance
Lightning Source LLC
Chambersburg PA
CBHW042004150426
43194CB00002B/118